Erratic
"A Little Bit of Everything"
Grayscale Coloring Book

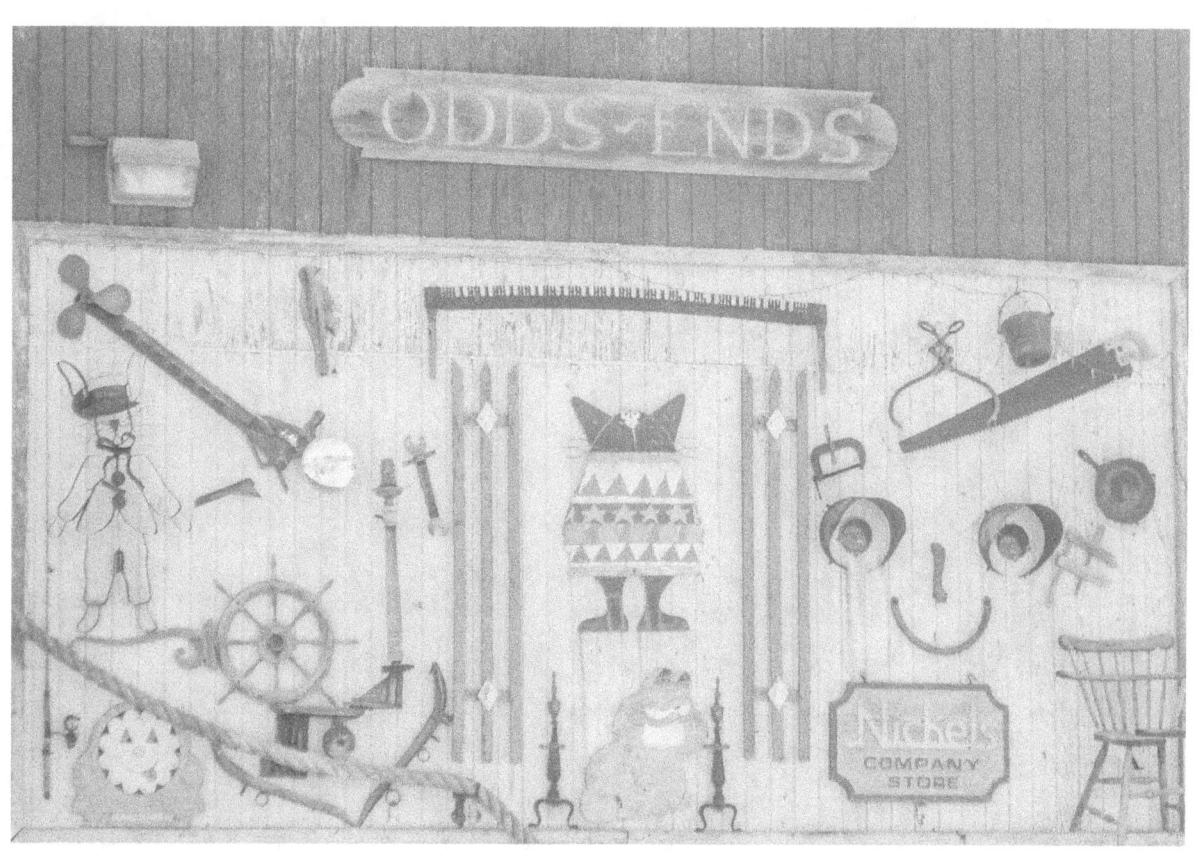

Madeline Rose

Erratic is a collection of photographs taken by me, a college student and photographer, for my second Grayscale coloring book. It is a collection of "a little bit of everything." I hope you enjoy coloring these pages as much as I enjoyed taking the pictures!

Madeline

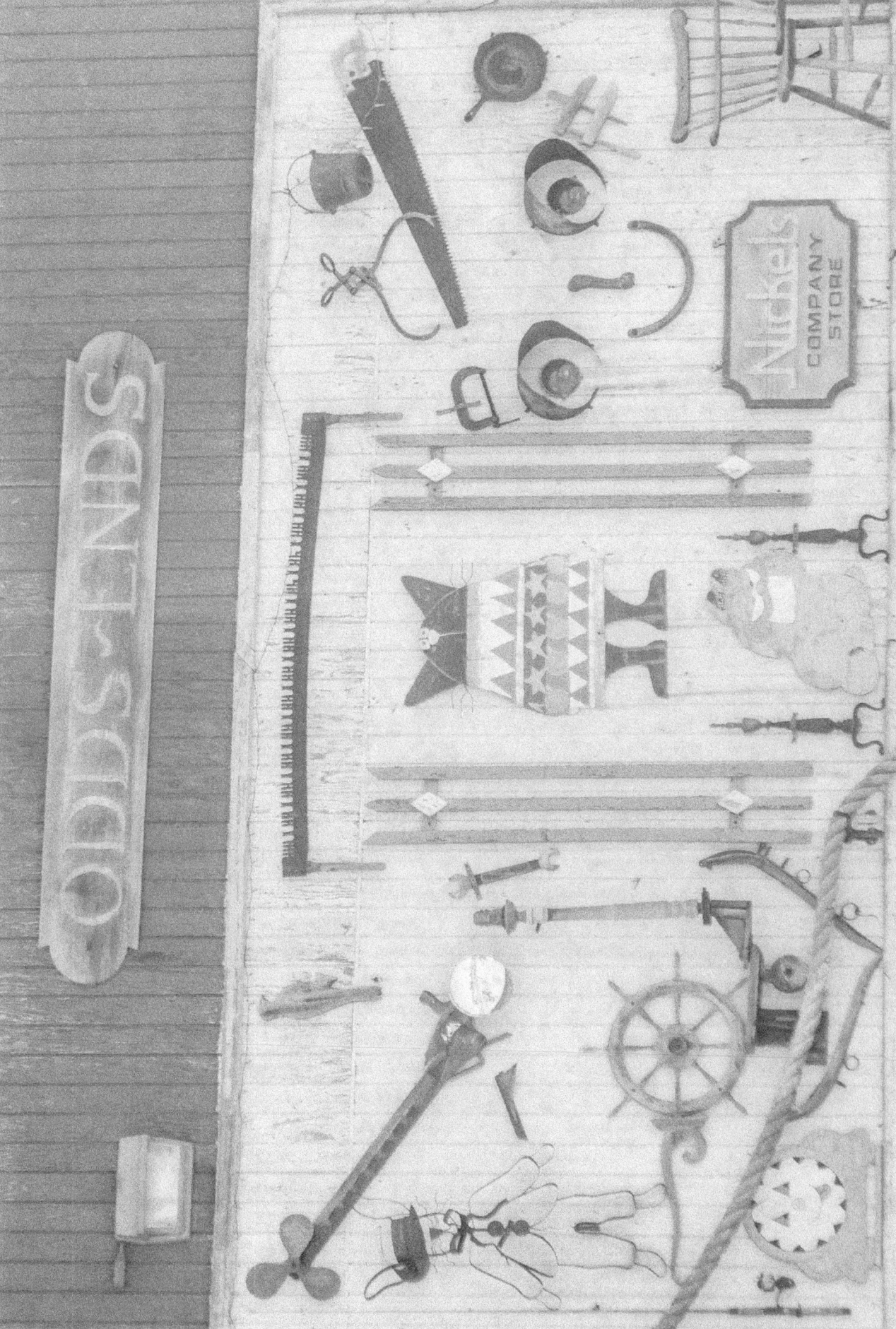

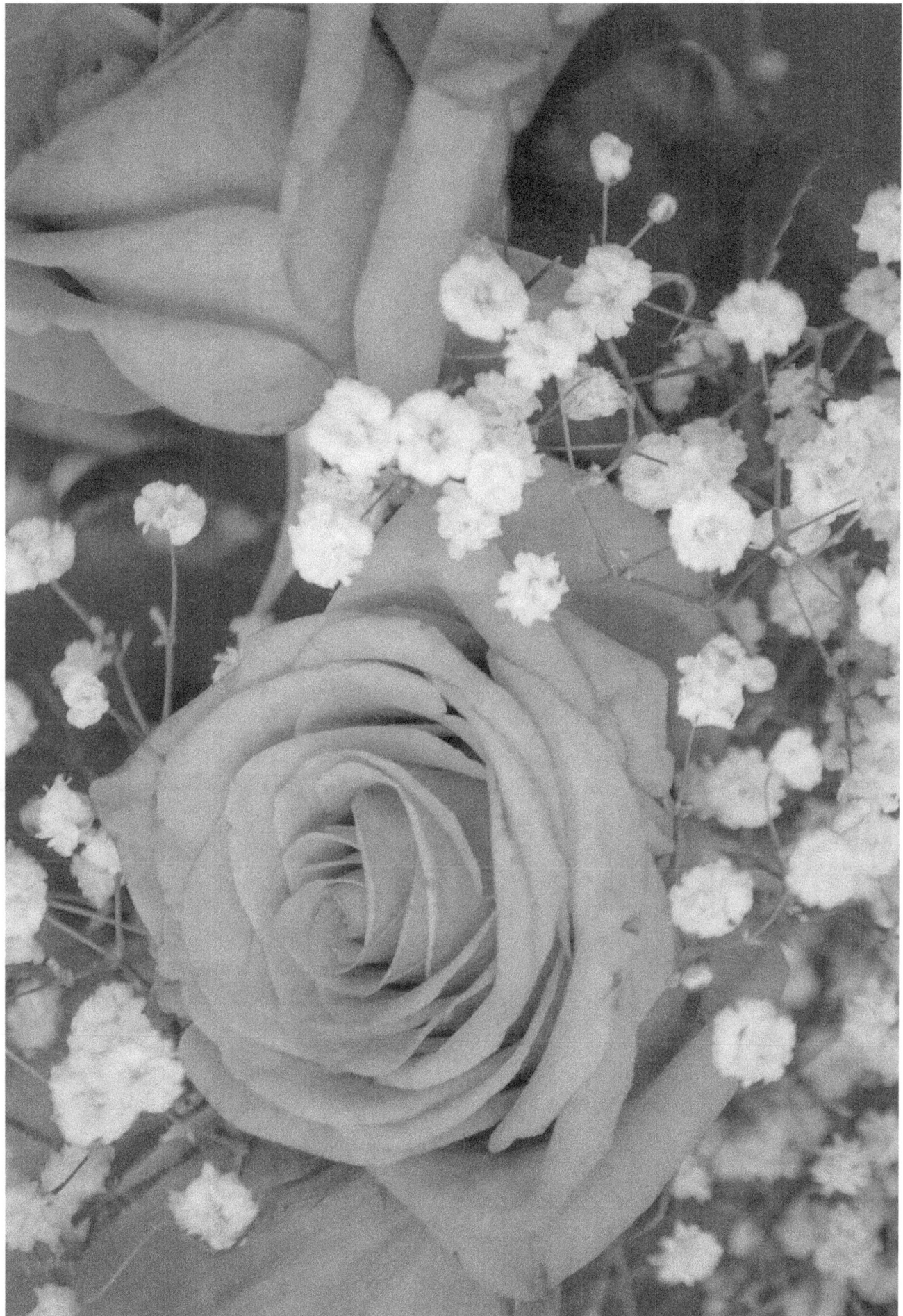

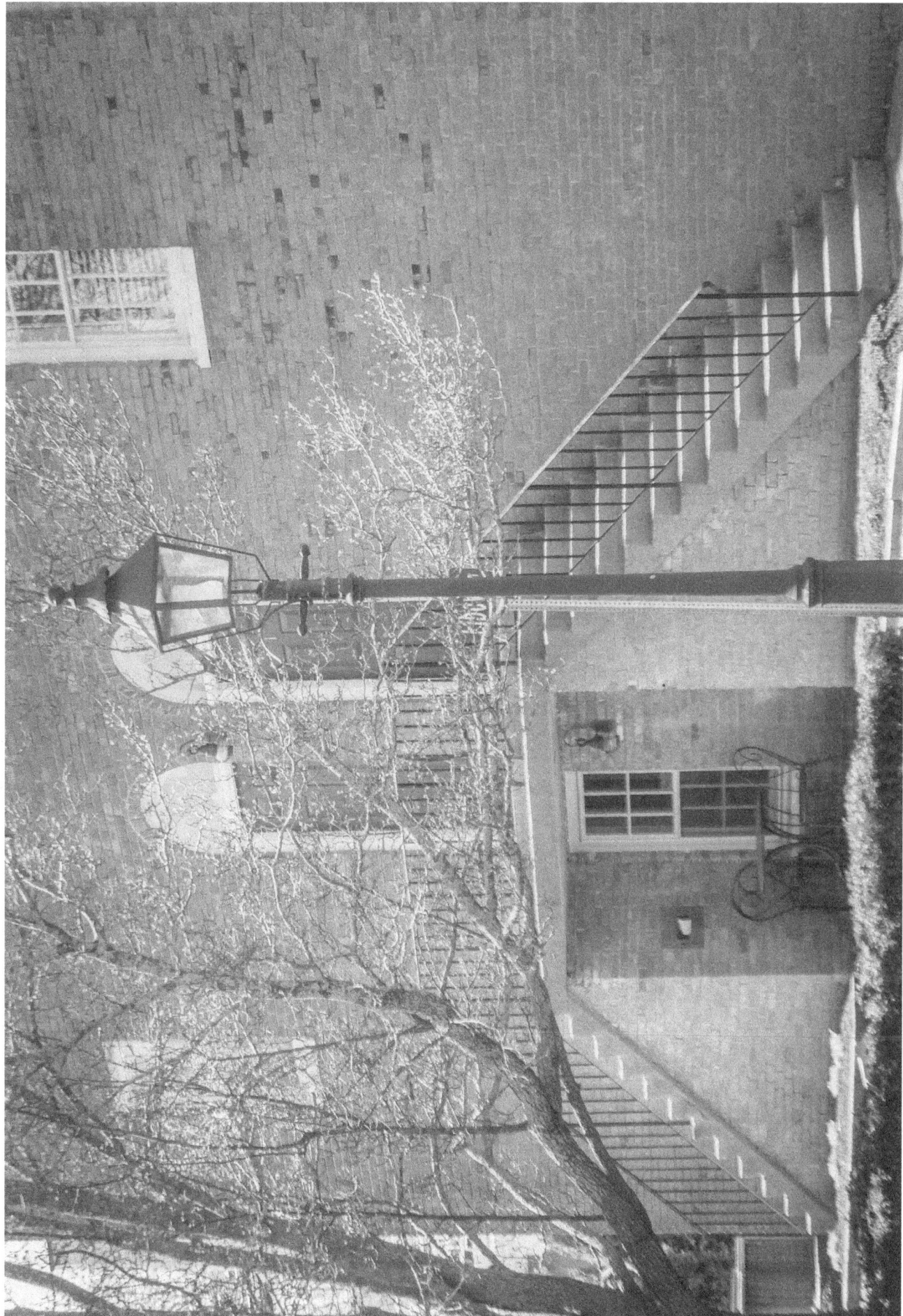

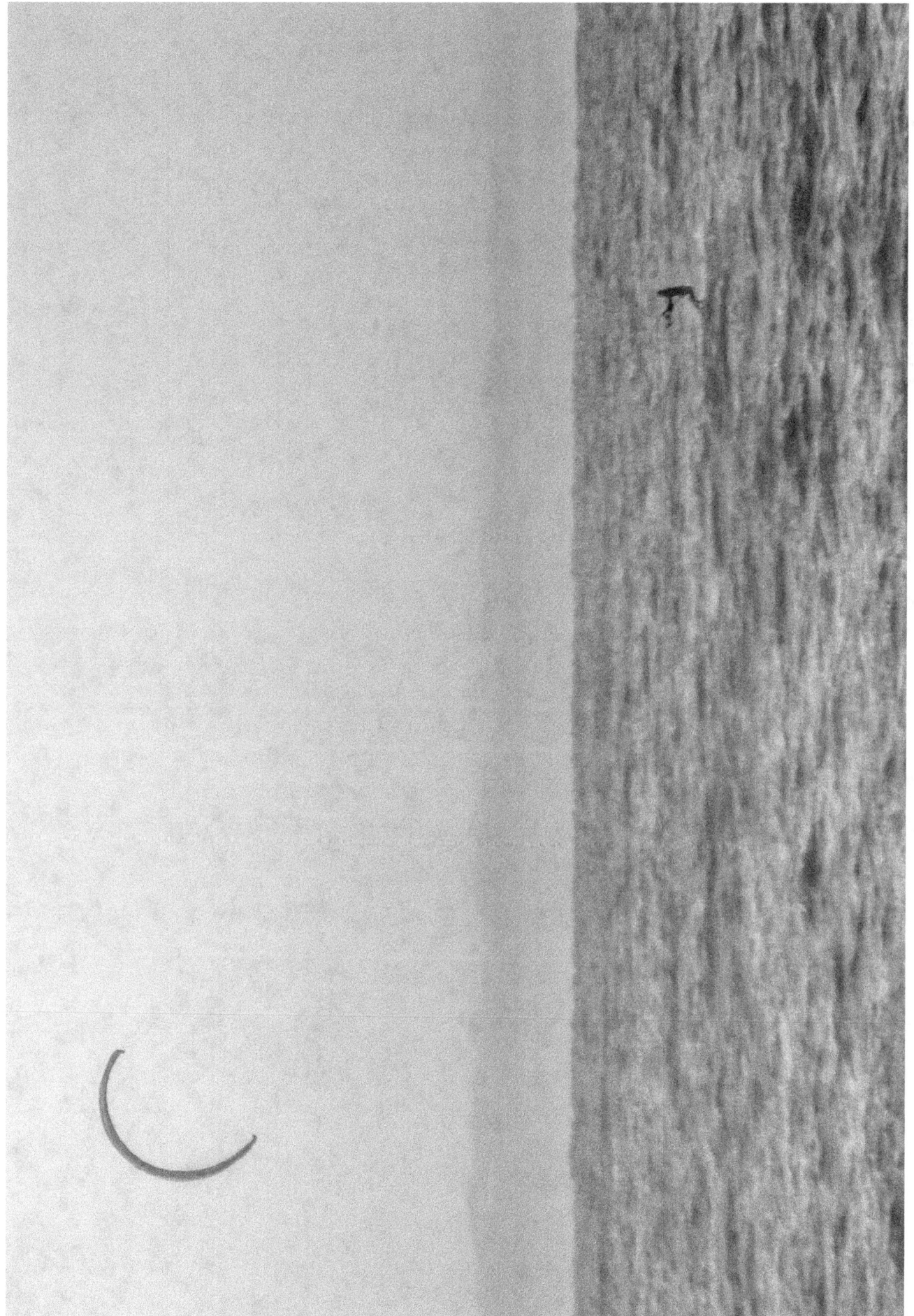

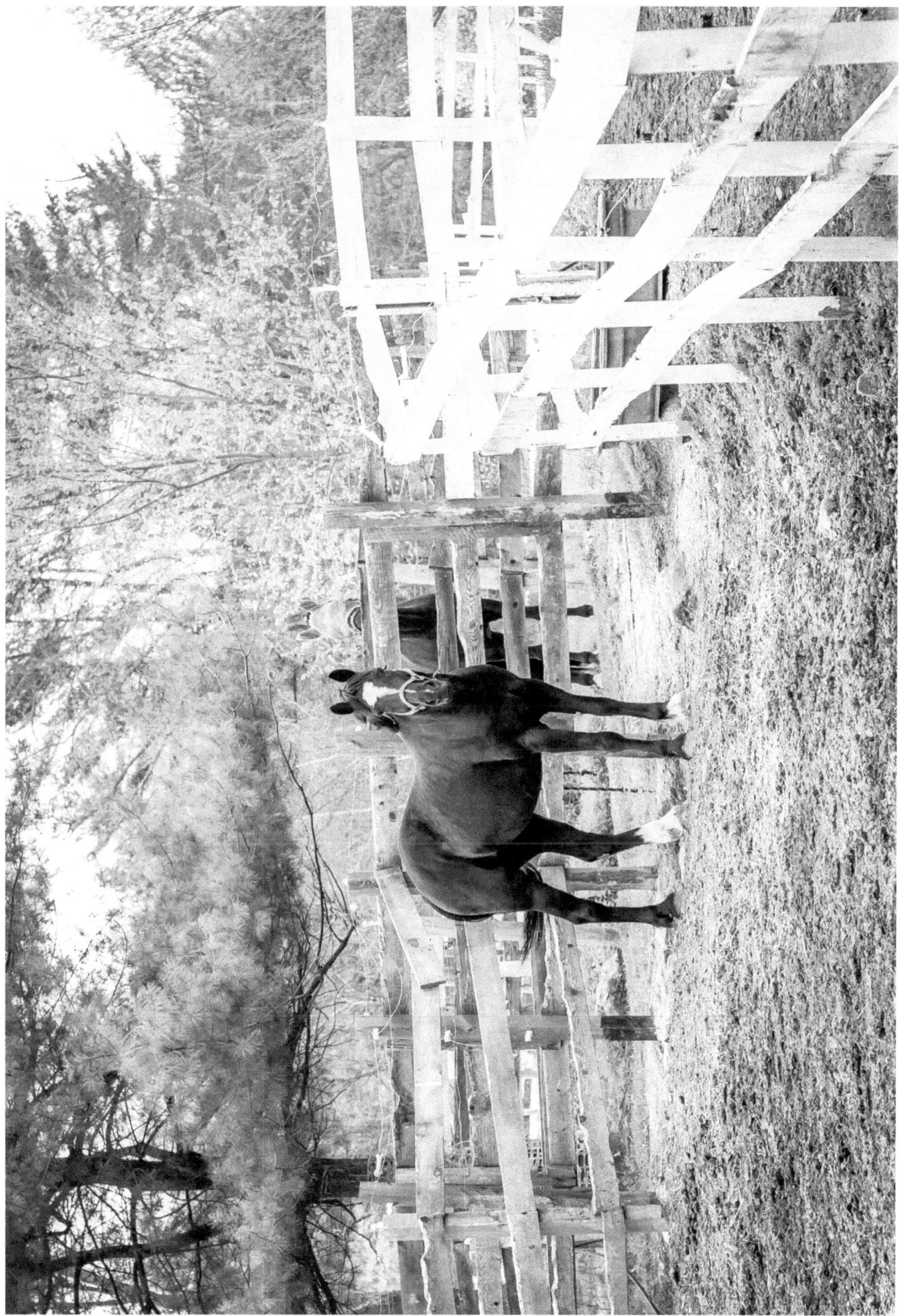

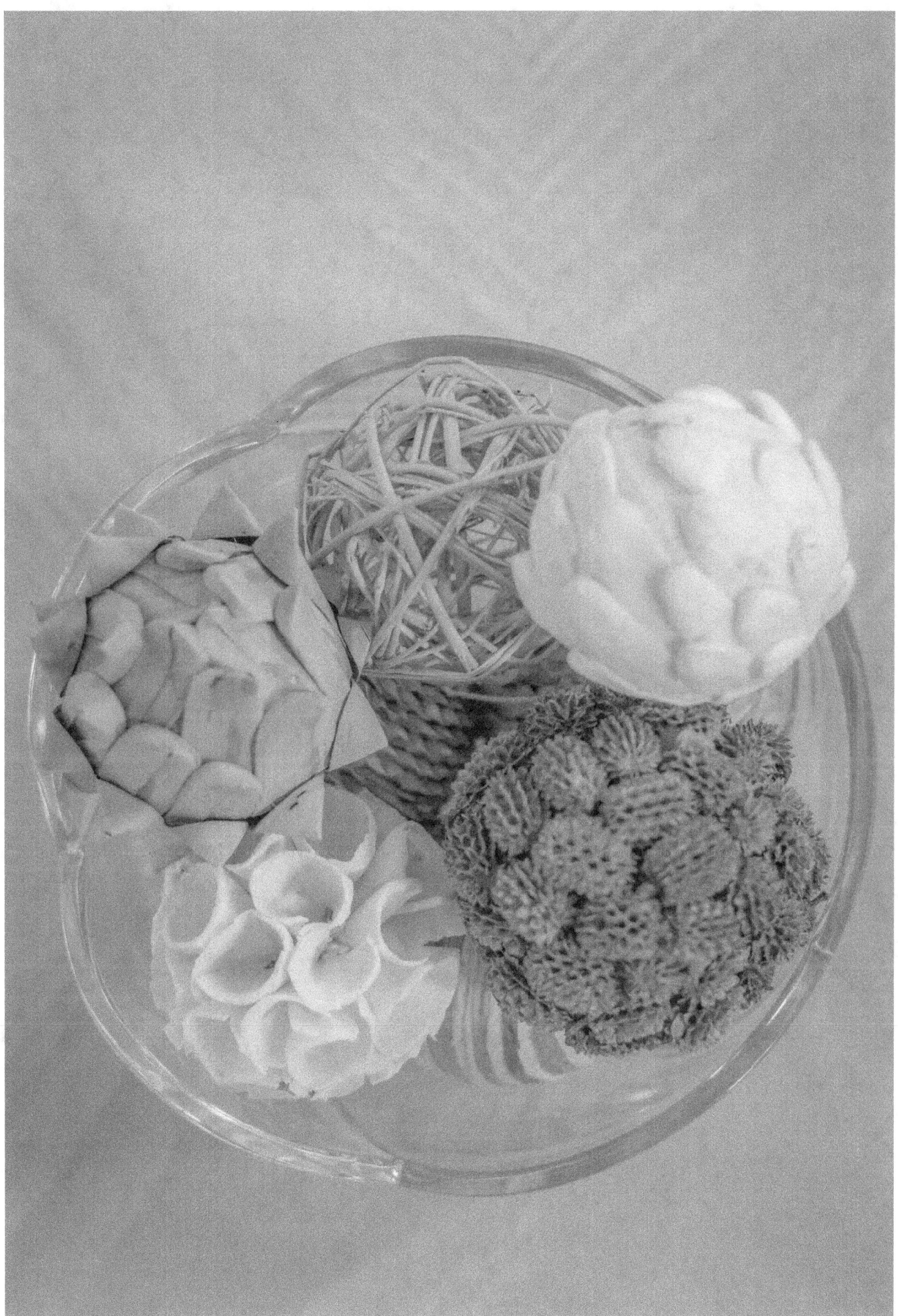

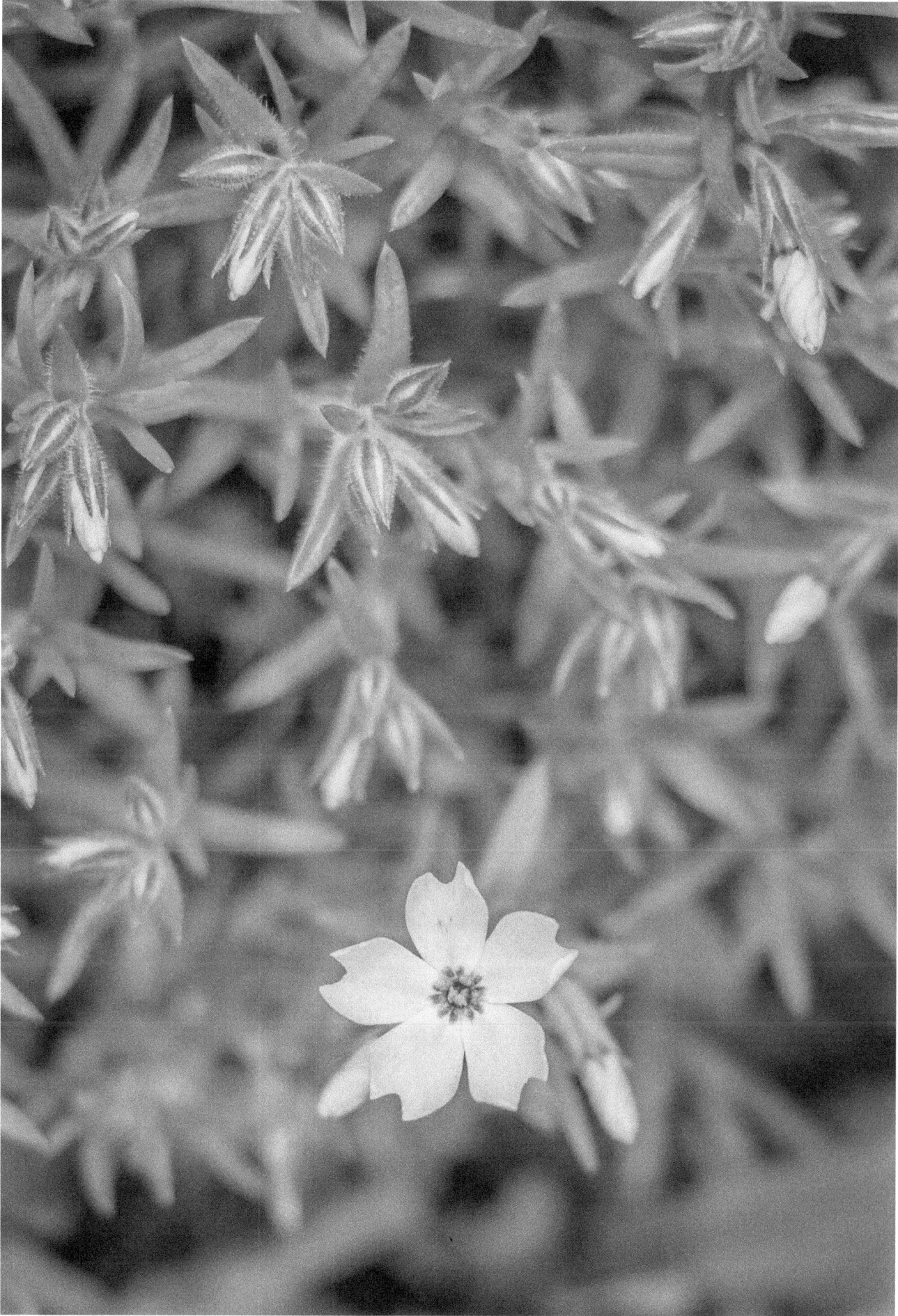

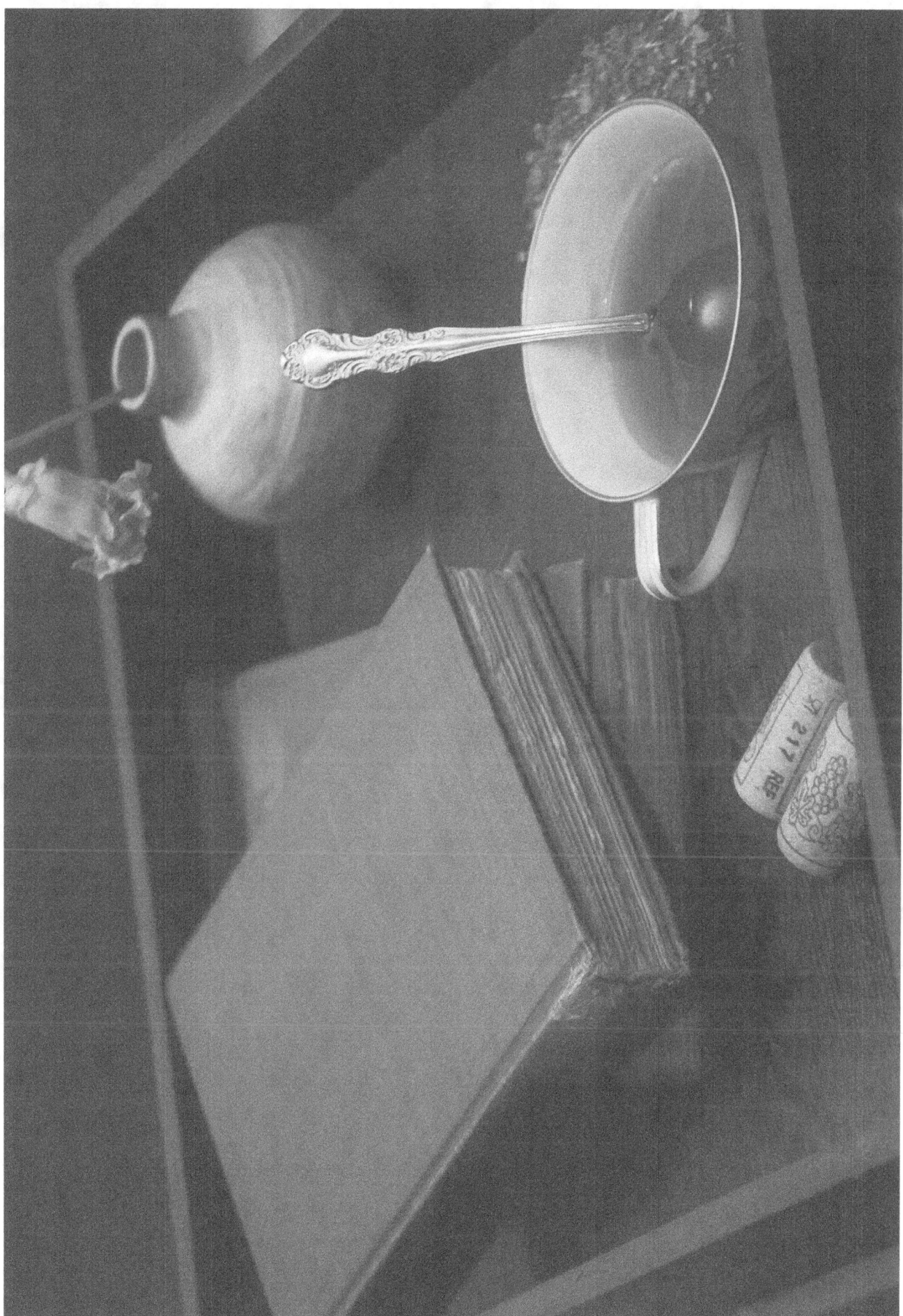

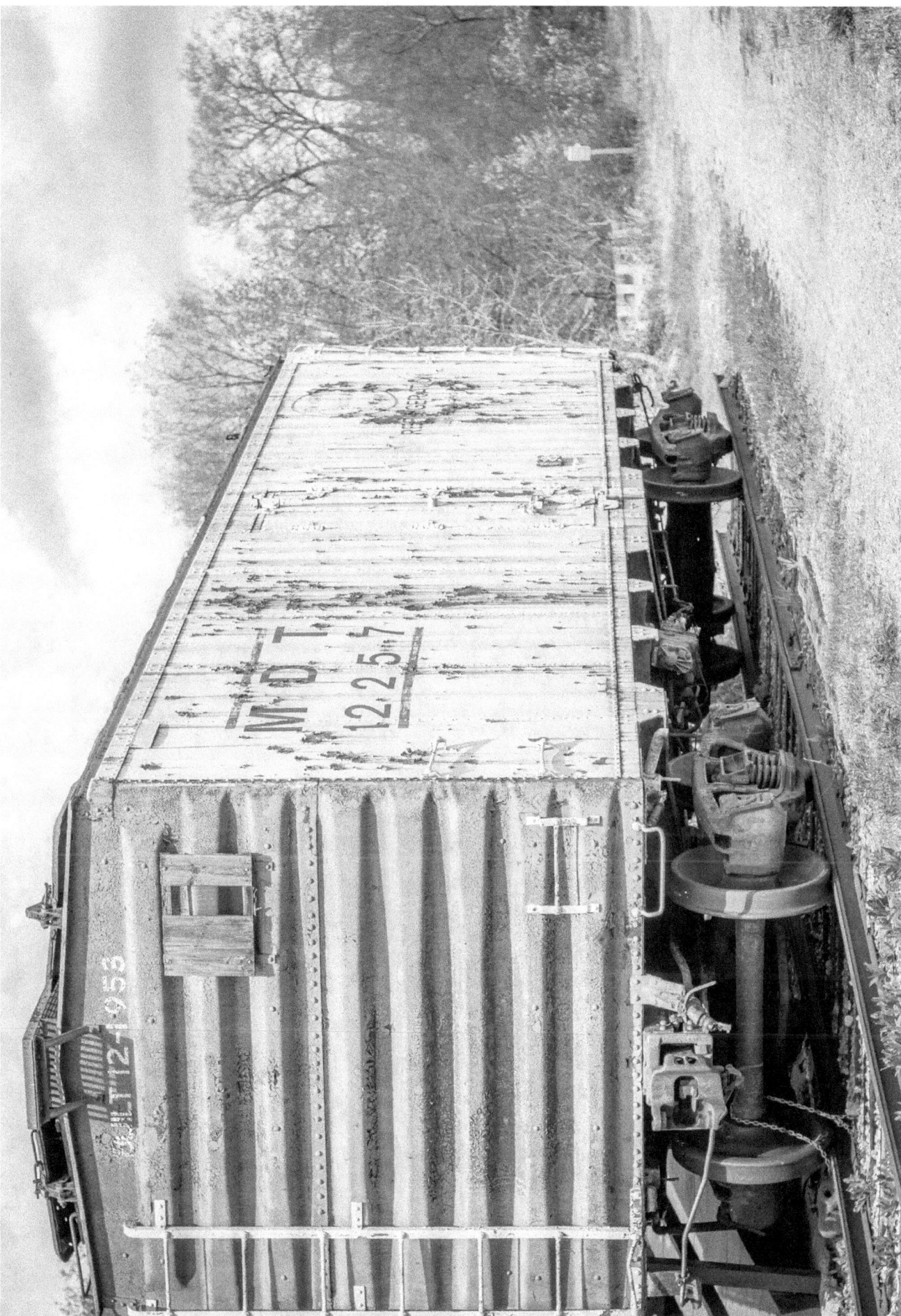

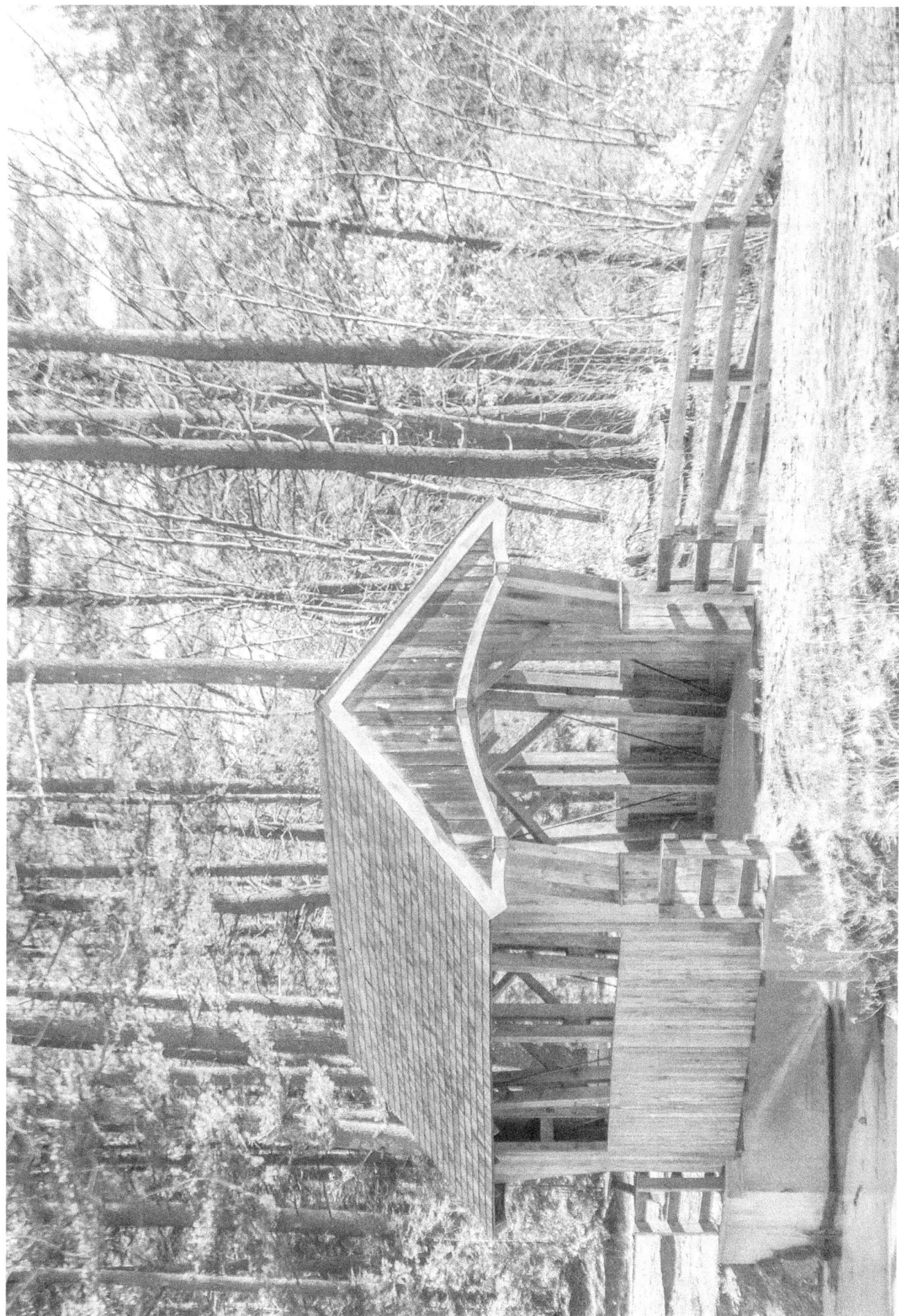

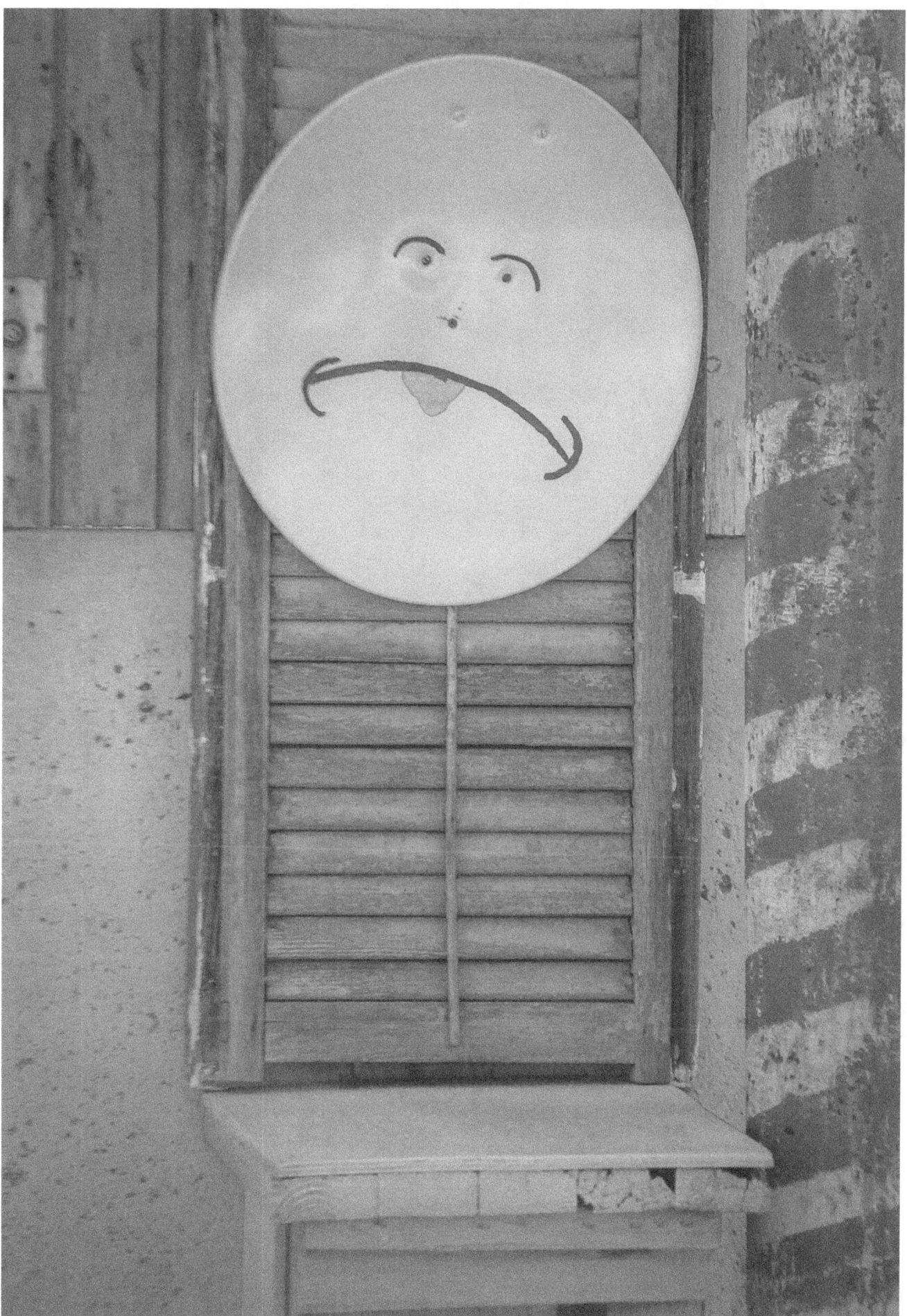

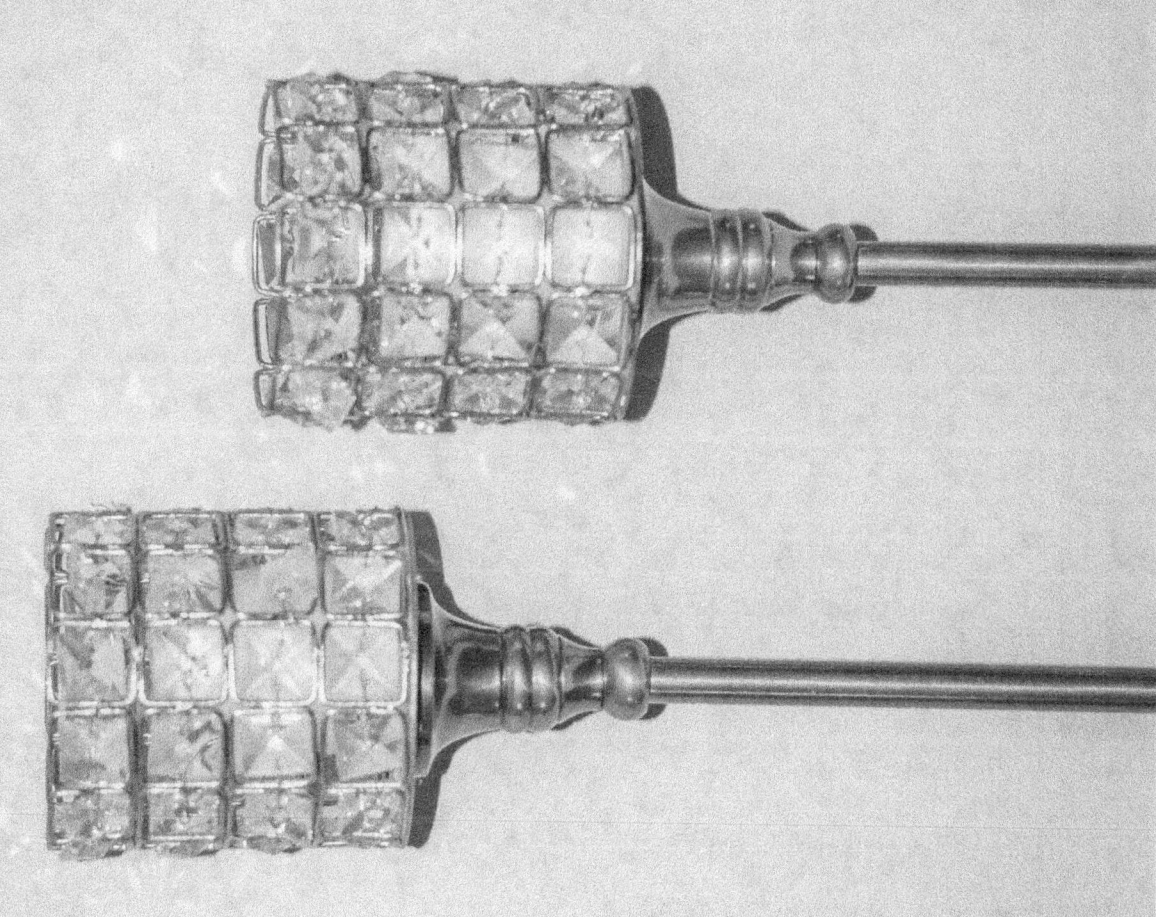

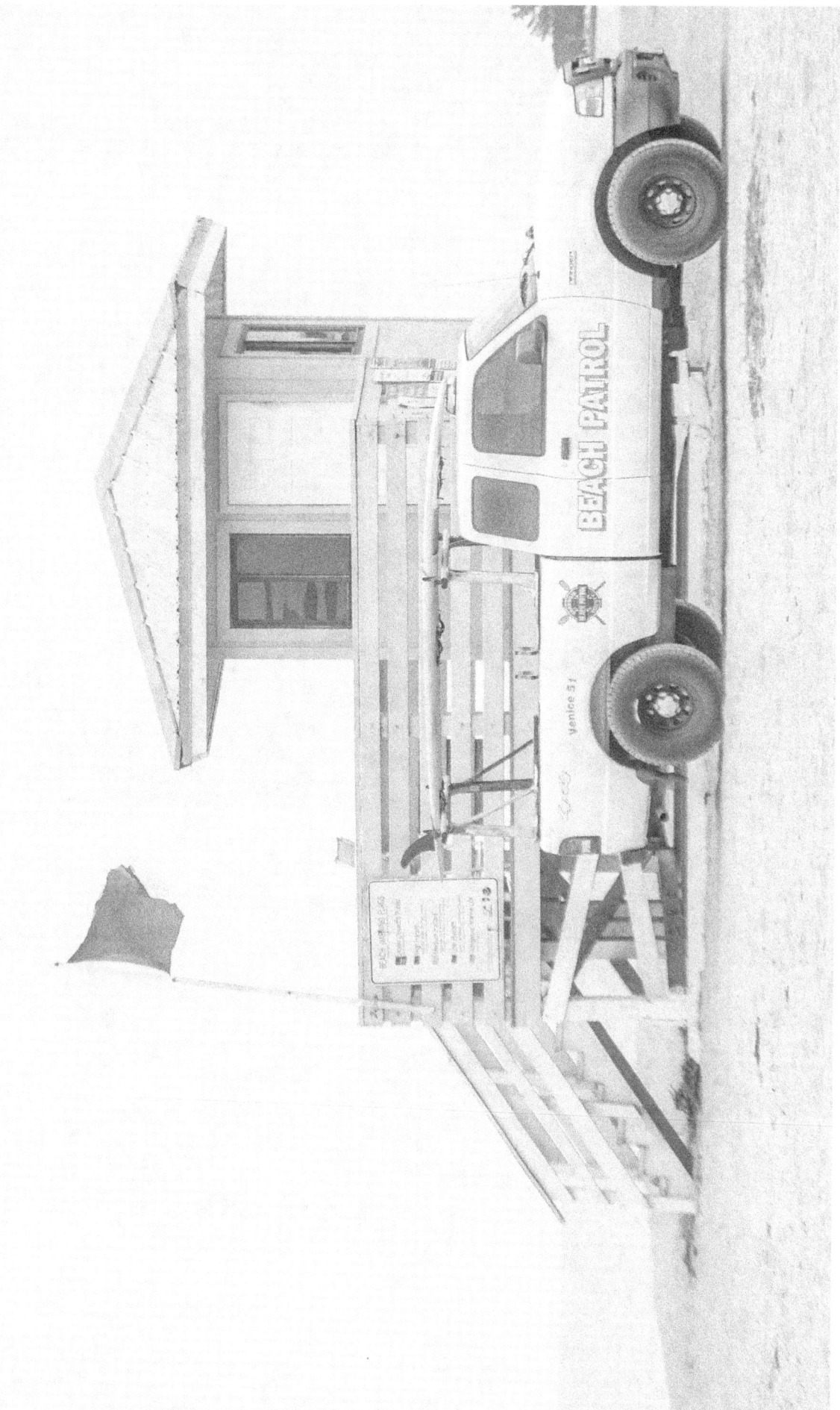

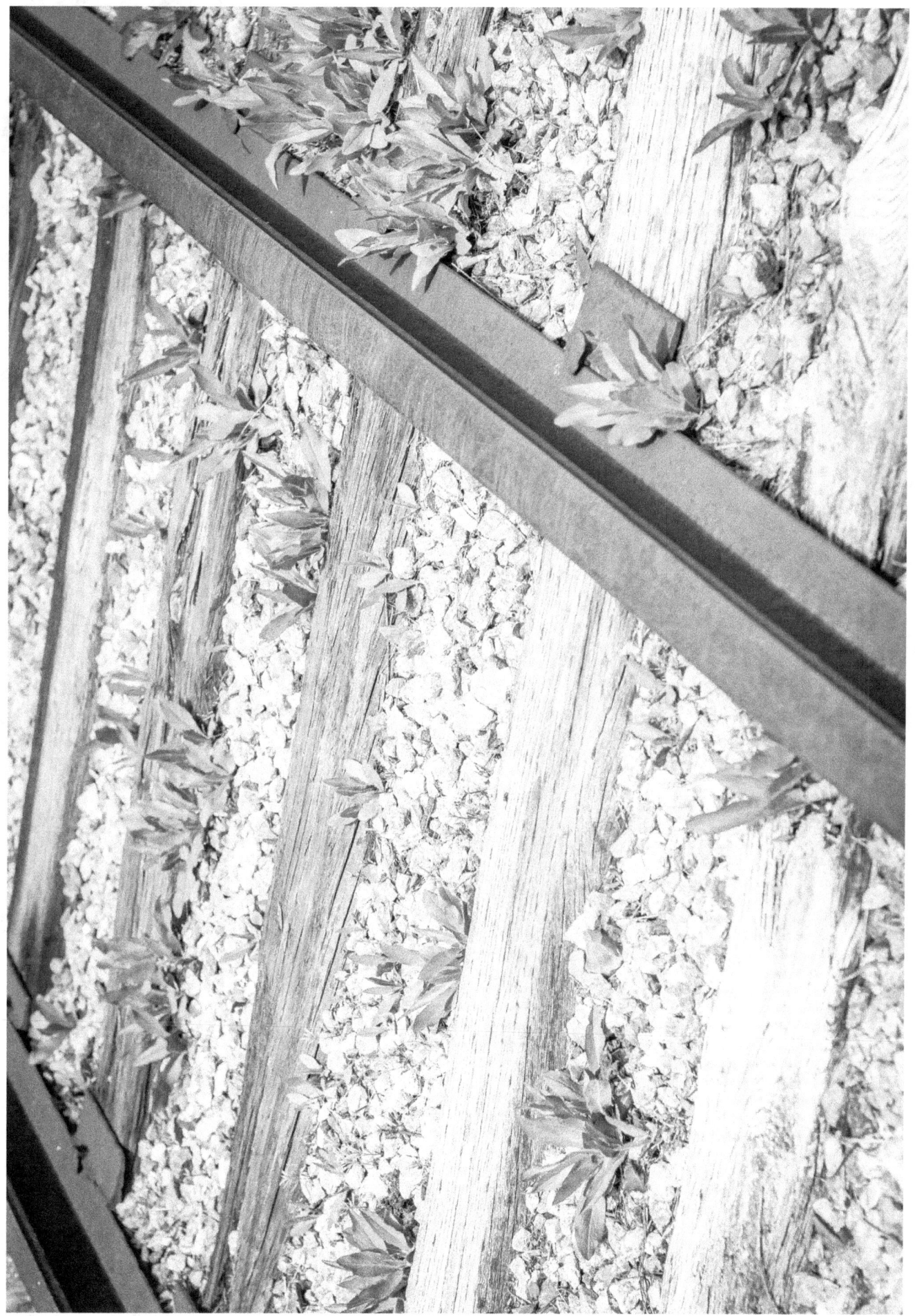

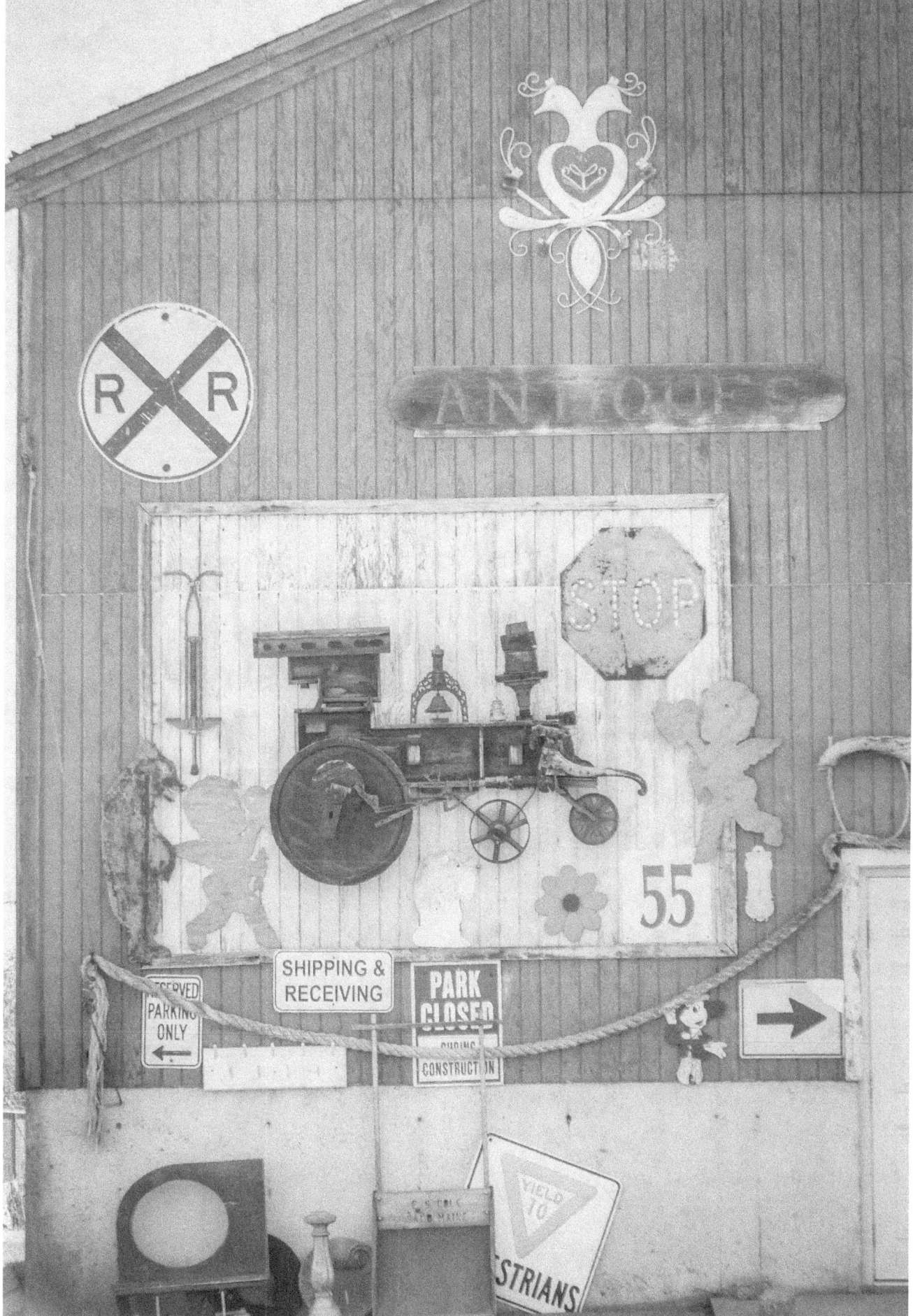

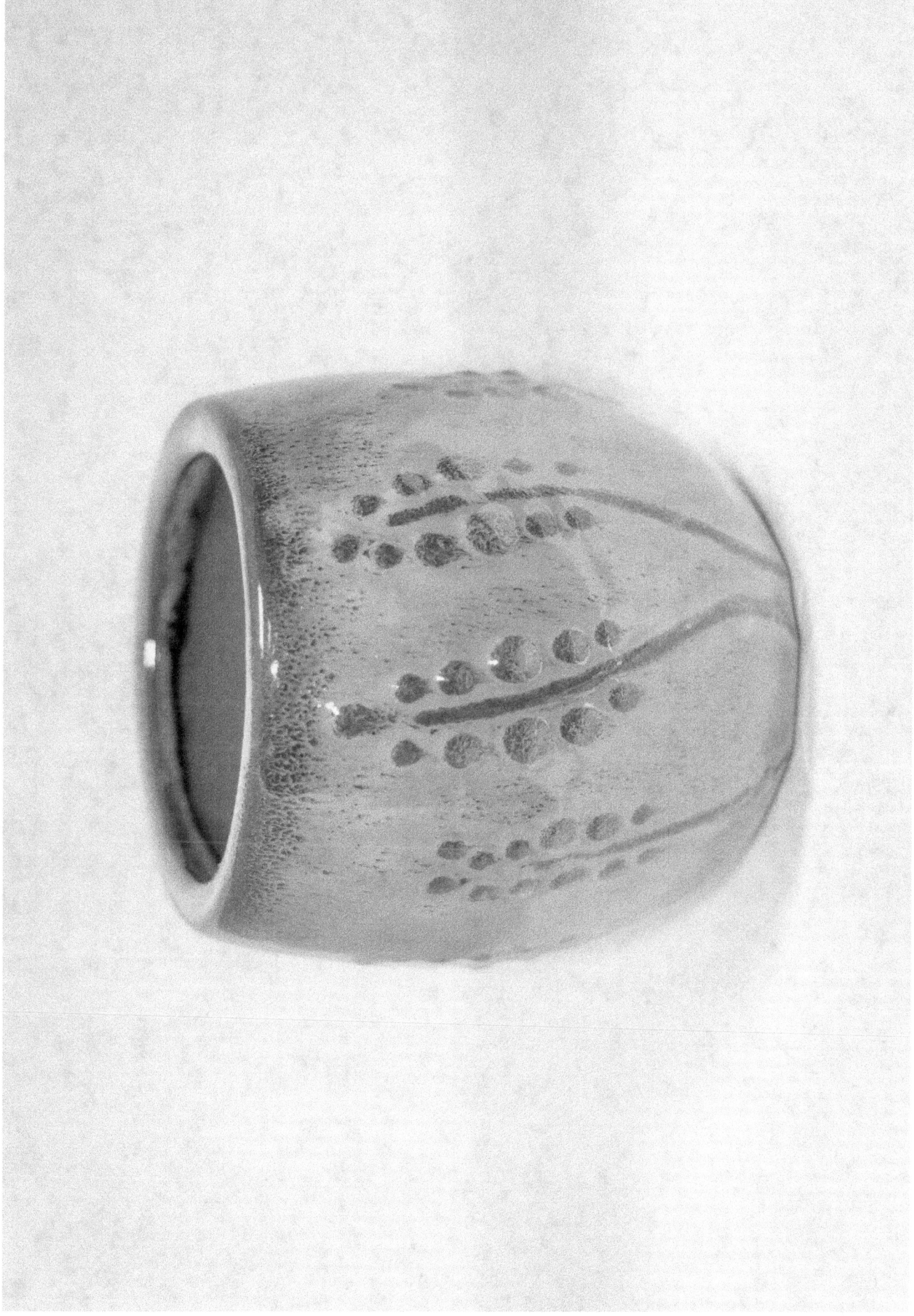

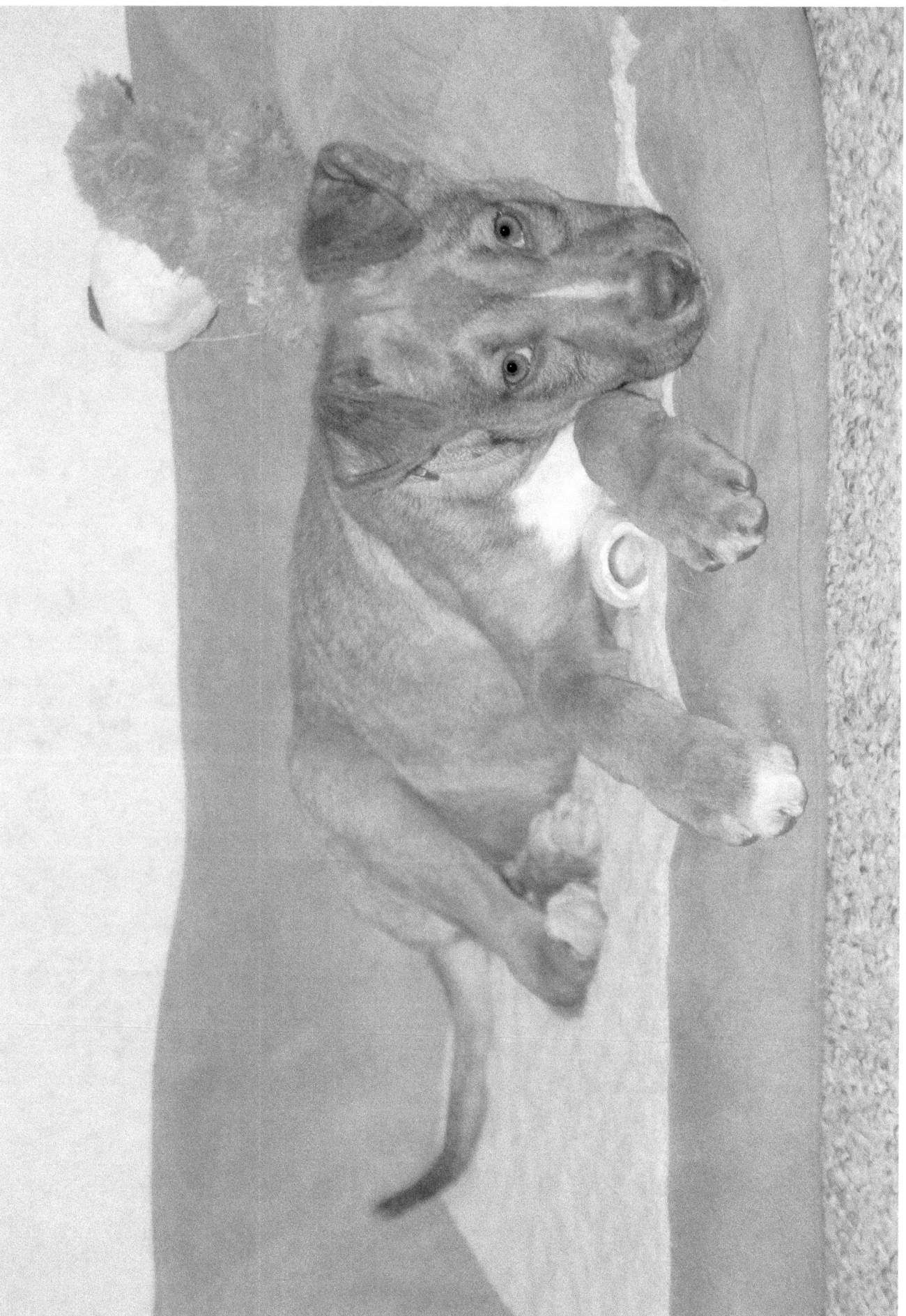

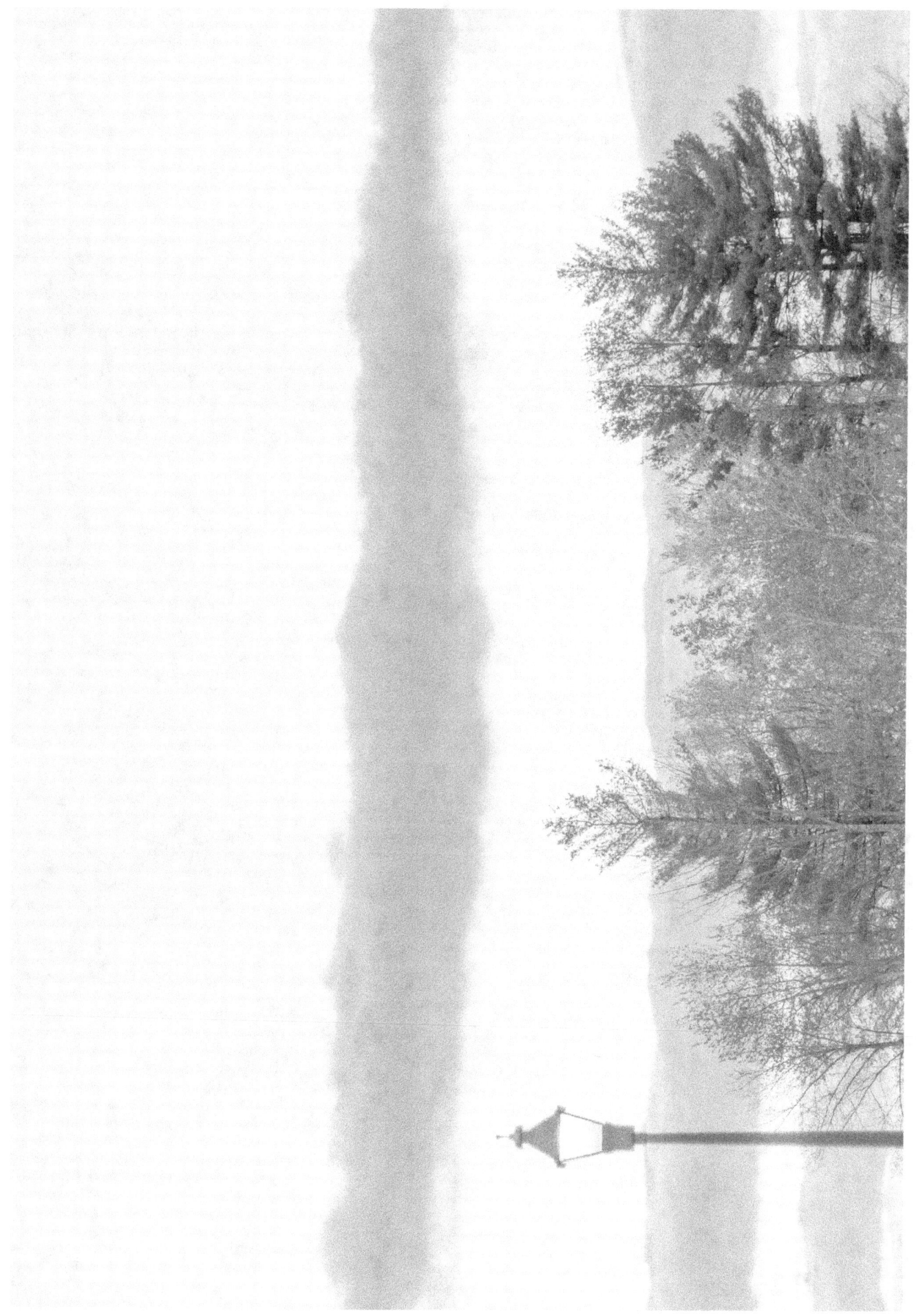

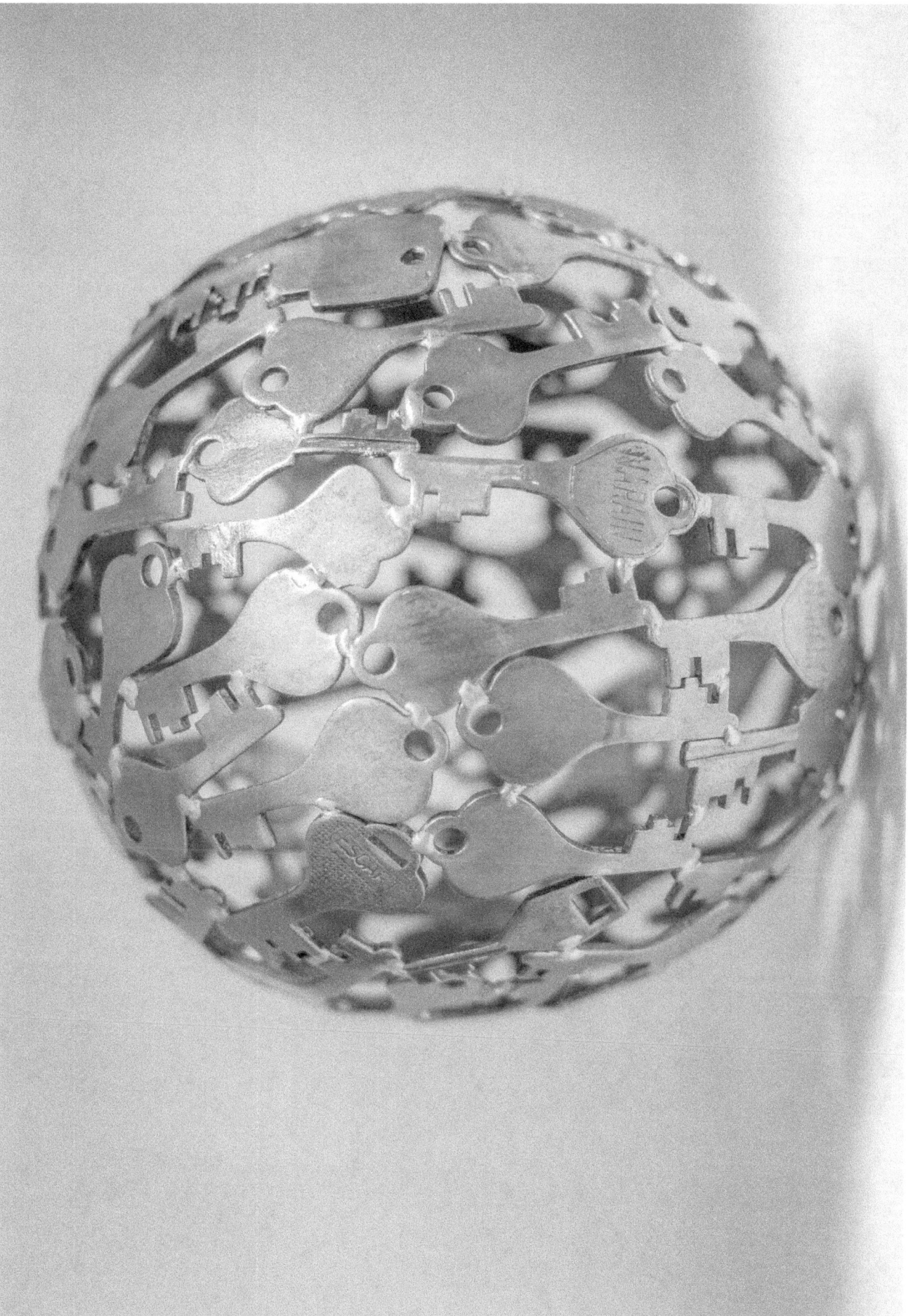

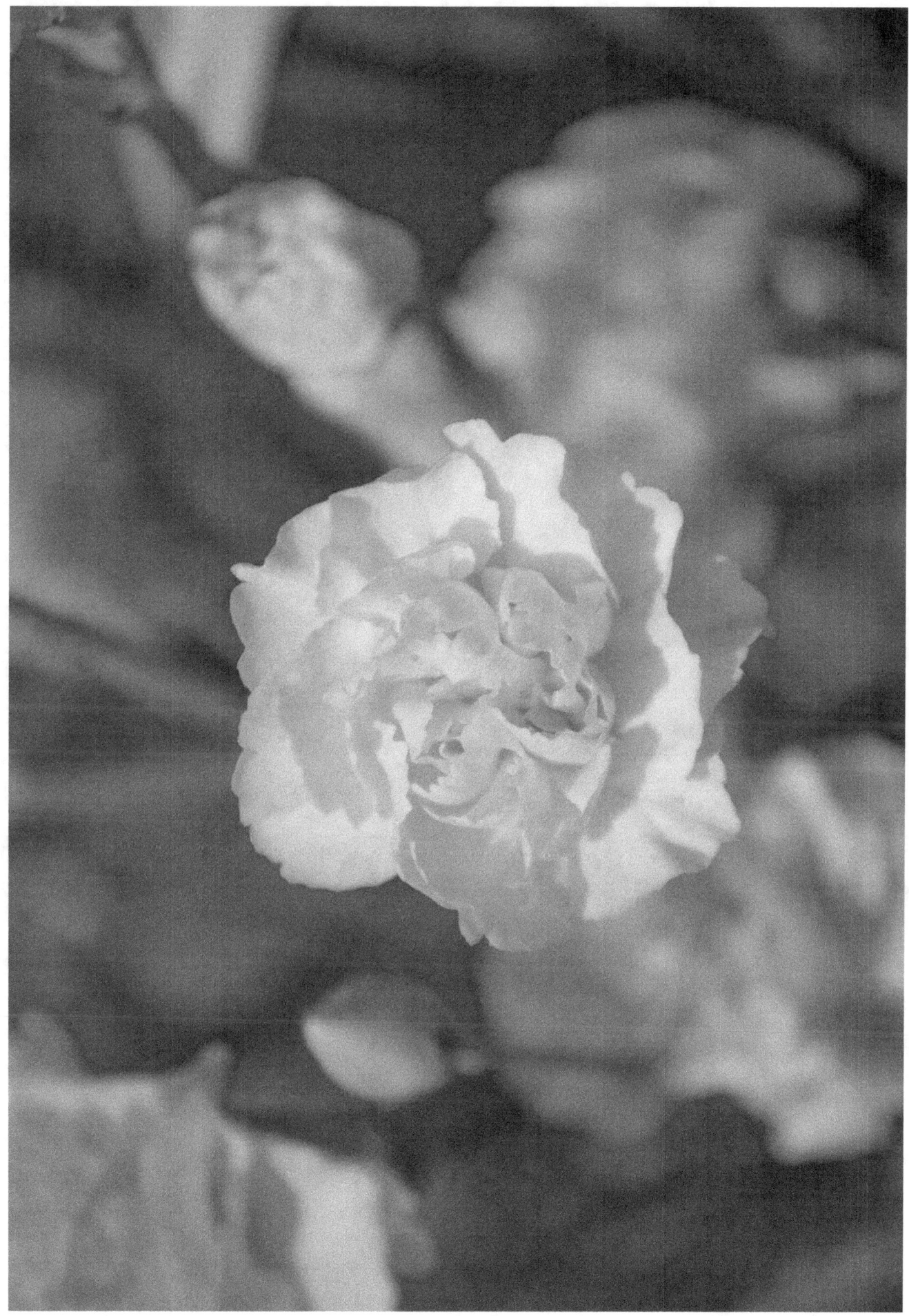